WOMEN

Extracts from the Writings of
Bahá'u'lláh, 'Abdu'l–Bahá,
Shoghi Effendi and the
Universal House of Justice

Compiled by:
The Research Department
of the Universal House of Justice

BAHÁ'Í CANADA PUBLICATIONS
Bahá'í National Centre/7200 Leslie Street/Thornhill, Ontario, Canada

ISBN 0-88867-045-1

Printed in Canada

Contents

I.

The Concept of Equality

Extracts from the Writings of Bahá'u'lláh:

1. O Children of Men! Know ye not why We created you all from the same dust? That no one should exalt himself over the other. Ponder at all times in your hearts how ye were created. Since We have created you all from one same substance it is incumbent on you to be even as one soul, to walk with the same feet, eat with the same mouth and dwell in the same land, that from your inmost being, by your deeds and actions, the signs of oneness and the essence of detachment may be made manifest. Such is My counsel to you. O concourse of light! Heed ye this counsel that ye may obtain the fruit of holiness from the tree of wondrous glory.

(Hidden Words, U.K. 1949 edition, pages 19–20)

2. Exalted, immensely exalted is He Who hath removed differences and established harmony. Glorified, infinitely glorified is He Who hath caused discord to cease, and decreed solidarity and unity. Praised be God, the Pen of the Most High hath lifted distinctions from between His servants and hand maidens and, through His consummate favours and all–encompassing mercy, hath conferred upon all a station and rank on the same plane. He hath broken the back of vain imaginings with the sword of utterance and hath obliterated the perils of idle fancies through the pervasive power of His might.

(Extract from previously untranslated Tablet)

3. O My handmaiden, My leaf! This Wronged One hath heard thy voice and that which thy inner and outer tongue hath uttered in praise of thy Lord. By the righteousness of God! That which the people possess, and the treasures of the earth, and that which the rulers and kings own, are not equal in this day to the singing of His praise. The Lord of the Kingdom beareth witness unto this at this glorious moment. And having heard thy groaning and lamentation, We are responding with a Tablet which calleth out betwixt earth and heaven and maketh mention of thee with words that immortalize what hath appeared from thee in His love, in His service, in His remembrance

and in His praise. And He hath made that which hath issued forth from thy mouth a trust with Him for thee. He is verily the Most Bounteous, the Most Generous. If thou truly givest ear to that which hath been revealed for thee from My Supreme Pen at this moment, thou shalt soar with the wings of eagerness in the heaven of love for the Lord of the Day of the Covenant, and wilt say during all the days of thy life: Thanks be unto Thee, O Thou the Desire of the world, and praise be unto Thee, O Thou the Beloved of the people of understanding. May all existence be a sacrifice for Thy favour, and all that hath been and will ever be, a ransom for Thy Word, O Thou the Wronged One amongst the people of enmity, O Thou in Whose grasp are the reins of all who are in heaven and on earth. . . .

In this Day the Hand of divine grace hath removed all distinction. The servants of God and His handmaidens are regarded on the same plane. Blessed is the servant who hath attained unto that which God hath decreed, and likewise the leaf moving in accordance with the breezes of His will. This favour is great and this station lofty. His bounties and bestowals are ever present and manifest. Who is able to offer befitting gratitude for His successive bestowals and continuous favours?

(Extract from previously untranslated Tablet)

4. By My Life, the names of handmaidens who are devoted to God are written and set down by the Pen of the Most High in the Crimson Book. They excel over men in the sight of God. How numerous are the heroes and knights in the field who are bereft of the True One and have no share in His recognition, but thou hast attained and received thy fill.

(Extract from previously untranslated Tablet)

5. He is the All-Seeing from the Horizon of the Heaven of Knowledge! O My handmaiden, O My leaf! Verily the Pen of the Most High hath borne witness unto thy recognition of Him, thy love for Him and thy turning towards the Ancient Countenance at a time when the world hath rejected Him, save those whom God, the Most High, hath willed. . . .

Well is it with thee for having adorned thyself with the ornament of the love of God and for having been enabled to make mention of Him and utter His praise. Divine grace, in its entirety, is in the mighty grasp of God, exalted be He. He conferreth it upon whomsoever He willeth. How many a man considered himself a celebrated divine and a repository of heavenly mysteries, and yet when the slightest test visited him, he arose with such opposition and denial as to cause the Concourse on high to moan and lament. Through the bestowals of the Lord, however, and His infinite favour, thou hast attained unto the hidden secret and the well-guarded treasure. Preserve then, in the name of God, this lofty station and conceal it from the eyes of betrayers. The glory shining from the horizon of My Kingdom be upon thee and upon every handmaiden who hath attained the splendours of My sublime Throne.

(Extract from previously untranslated Tablet)

6. . . . We beseech God to aid all the leaves to attain the knowledge of the Tree and deprive them not of the ocean of His generosity. In this day no regard is paid to loftiness or lowliness, to poverty or wealth, to nobility and lineage, to weakness or might. Whosoever recognizeth the incomparable Beloved is the possessor of true wealth and occupieth a divine station. Today, in the court of the True One, the queen of the world and her like are not worth a mustard seed, because although she may speak in the name of God, invoke the Lord of creation every day in the temple of her body, and spend large sums of earthly wealth for the development of her nation, she is deprived of recognition of the Sun of His Manifestation and is barred from the True One in Whose remembrance she is engaged.

(Extract from previously untranslated Tablet)

7. He is effulgent from the all-highest Horizon. O My handmaid! Throughout the centuries and ages many a man hath waited expectant for God's Revelation, and yet when the Light shone forth from the horizon of the world, all but a few turned their faces away from it. Whosoever from amongst the handmaidens hath recognized the Lord of all Names is recorded in the Book as one of those men [1] by the Pen of the Most High. Offer thou praise to the Beloved of the world for having aided thee to recognize the Dayspring of His Signs and the Revealer of the evidences of His Glory. This is a great bounty, a bounteous favour. Preserve it in the name of the True One . . . .

(Extract from previously untranslated Tablet)

---

1. It is clear from other extracts that the Bahá'í concept of equality implies complementarity not uniformity with men.

Extracts from the Writings and Utterances of 'Abdu'l-Bahá:

8. ...From the beginning of existence until the Promised Day men retained superiority over women in every respect. It is revealed in the Qur'án: "Men have superiority over women." But in this wondrous Dispensation, the supreme outpouring of the Glorious Lord became the cause of manifest achievements by women. Some handmaidens arose who excelled men in the arena of knowledge. They arose with such love and spirituality that they became the cause of the outpouring of the bounty of the Sovereign Lord upon mankind, and with their sanctity, purity and attributes of the spirit led a great many to the shore of unity. They became a guiding torch to the wanderers in the wastes of bewilderment, and enkindled the despondent in the nether world with the flame of the love of the Lord. This is a bounteous characteristic of this wondrous Age which hath granted strength to the weaker sex and hath bestowed masculine might upon womanhood....

(Extract from previously untranslated Tablet)

9. O handmaid of God! In this wondrous dispensation in which the Ancient Beauty and the Manifest Light—may my spirit be sacrificed for His loved ones—hath risen from the horizon of age-old hopes, women have assumed the attributes of men in showing forth steadfastness in the Cause of God, and revealing the heroism and might of fearless men. They invaded the arena of mystic knowledge and hoisted aloft the banner on the heights of certitude. Thou, too, must make a mighty effort and show forth supreme courage. Exert thyself and taste of the sweetness of a heavenly draught, for the sweet taste of the love of God will linger on to the end that hath no end.

(Extract from previously untranslated Tablet)

10. O handmaid of God! Render thanks to the Lord that among that

5

race[2] thou art the first believer, that thou hast engaged in spreading sweet-scented breezes, and hast arisen to guide others. It is my hope that through the bounties and favours of the Abhá Beauty thy countenance may be illumined, thy disposition pleasing, and thy fragrance diffused, that thine eyes may be seeing, thine ears attentive, thy tongue eloquent, thy heart filled with supreme glad-tidings, and thy soul refreshed by divine fragrances, so that thou mayest arise among that race and occupy thyself with the edification of the people, and become filled with light. Although the pupil of the eye is black, it is the source of light. Thou shalt likewise be. The disposition should be bright not the appearance. Therefore, with supreme confidence and certitude, say: "O God! Make me a radiant light, a shining lamp, and a brilliant star, so that I may illumine the hearts with an effulgent ray from Thy Kingdom of Abhá. . . ."

(Extract from previously untranslated Tablet)

11. The establishment of a women's assemblage for the promotion of knowledge is entirely acceptable, but discussions must be confined to educational matters. It should be done in such a way that differences will, day by day, be entirely wiped out, not that, God forbid, it will end in argumentation between men and women. As in the question of the veil, nothing should be done contrary to wisdom. The individual women should, today, follow a course of action which will be the cause of eternal glory to all womankind, so that all women will be illumined. And that lieth in gathering to learn how to teach, in holding meetings to recite the verses, to offer supplications to the kingdom of the Lord of evident signs, and to institute education for the girls. Ponder the manner in which Jináb-i-Ṭáhirih used to teach. She was free from every concern, and for this reason she was resplendent.

Now the world of women should be a spiritual world, not a political one, so that it will be radiant. The women of other nations are all im-

---

2. This Tablet was addressed to one Mrs. Pocahontas in Washington. According to Fáḍil Mázandarání, the recipient of the Tablet was a black woman. See "Táríkh̲-i-Ẓuhúru'l-Ḥaq", volume 8, Part 2, p. 1209 (Ṭihrán: Bahá'í Publishing Trust, 132 B.E.) Additional information provided by the Archives of the National Spiritual Assembly of the United States indicates that Mr. Louis Gregory, in a history of the Washington D.C. Bahá'í community, mentions a black Bahá'í, Mrs. Pocohontas Pope, who is very likely the same person. Mrs. Pope learned of the Bahá'í Faith through Alma and Fanny Knobloch and Joseph and Pauline Hannen. There is, at present, no other information on Mrs. Pope.

mersed in political matters. Of what benefit is this, and what fruit
doth it yield? To the extent that ye can, ye should busy yourselves
with spiritual matters which will be conducive to the exaltation of the
Word of God and of the diffusion of His fragrances. Your demeanour
should lead to harmony amongst all and to coalescence and the good-
pleasure of all. . . . [3]

I am endeavouring, with Bahá'u'lláh's confirmations and
assistance, so to improve the world of the handmaidens that all will
be astonished. This progress is intended to be in spirituality, in virtues, in human perfections and in divine knowledge. In America, the
cradle of women's liberation, women are still debarred from political
institutions because they squabble. . . . Ye need to be calm and com-
posed, so that the work will proceed with wisdom, otherwise there
will be such chaos that ye will leave everything and run away. "This
newly born babe is traversing in one night the path that needeth a hun-
dred years to tread." In brief, ye should now engage in matters of
pure spirituality and not contend with men. 'Abdu'l-Bahá will tact-
fully take appropriate steps. Be assured. In the end thou wilt thyself
exclaim, "This was indeed supreme wisdom!" I appeal to you to
obliterate this contention between men and women. . . .

No one can on his own achieve anything. 'Abdu'l-Bahá must be
well pleased and assist.

(Extract from previously untranslated Tablet)

12. Know thou, O handmaid, that in the sight of Bahá, women are
accounted the same as men, and God hath created all humankind in
His own image, and after His own likeness. That is, men and women
alike are the revealers of His names and attributes, and from the
spiritual viewpoint there is no difference between them. Whosoever
draweth nearer to God, that one is the most favoured, whether man
or woman. How many a handmaid, ardent and devoted, hath, within
the sheltering shade of Bahá, proved superior to the men, and surpassed the famous of the earth.

The House of Justice, however, according to the explicit text of the
Law of God, is confined to men;[4] this for a wisdom of the Lord

---

3. This advice was addressed to the Bahá'í women of Iran at that time. It is made
clear in other Tablets that, in principle, women are encouraged to take part in all
aspects of the life of society.

4. From other extracts it is evident that the limitation of membership to men applies
only to the Universal House of Justice, and not to the National and Local Houses of
Justice.

7

God's, which will ere long be made manifest as clearly as the sun at high noon.

(Selections from the Writings of 'Abdu'l-Bahá, 1978 World Centre edition, pp. 79–80)

13. And among the teachings of Bahá'u'lláh is the equality of women and men. The world of humanity has two wings—one is women and the other men. Not until both wings are equally developed can the bird fly. Should one wing remain weak, flight is impossible. Not until the world of women becomes equal to the world of men in the acquisition of virtues and perfections, can success and prosperity be attained as they ought to be.

(Selections from the Writings of 'Abdu'l-Bahá, 1978 World Centre edition, p. 302)

14. Inasmuch as this is the century of light, it is evident that the Sun of Reality, the Word, has revealed itself to all humankind. One of the potentialities hidden in the realm of humanity was the capability or capacity of womanhood. Through the effulgent rays of divine illumination the capacity of woman has become so awakened and manifest in this age that equality of man and woman is an established fact. . . .

In this day man must investigate reality impartially and without prejudice in order to reach the true knowledge and conclusions. What, then, constitutes the inequality between man and woman? Both are human. In powers and function each is the complement of the other. At most it is this: that woman has been denied the opportunities which man has so long enjoyed, especially the privilege of education. . . .

The truth is that all mankind are the creatures and servants of one God, and in His estimate all are human. *Man* is a generic term applying to all humanity. The biblical statement ''Let us make man in our image, after our likeness'' does not mean that woman was not created. The image and likeness of God apply to her as well. In Persian and Arabic there are two distinct words translated into English as man: one meaning man and woman collectively, the other distinguishing man as male from woman the female. The first word and its pronoun are generic, collective; the other is restricted to the male. This is the same in Hebrew.

To accept and observe a distinction which God has not intended in creation is ignorance and superstition. . . .

It is my hope that the banner of equality may be raised throughout the five continents where as yet it is not fully recognized and established. In this enlightened world of the West woman has advanced an immeasurable degree beyond the women of the Orient. And let it be known once more that until woman and man recognize and realize equality, social and political progress here or anywhere will not be possible. For the world of humanity consists of two parts or members: one is woman; the other is man. Until these two members are equal in strength, the oneness of humanity cannot be established, and the happiness and felicity of mankind will not be a reality. God willing, this is to be so.

(The Promulgation of Universal Peace, 1982 U.S. edition, pp. 74-77)

15. Today questions of the utmost importance are facing humanity, questions peculiar to this radiant century....

One of these questions concerns the rights of woman and her equality with man. In past ages it was held that woman and man were not equal—that is to say, woman was considered inferior to man, even from the standpoint of her anatomy and creation. She was considered especially inferior in intelligence, and the idea prevailed universally that it was not allowable for her to step into the arena of important affairs. In some countries man went so far as to believe and teach that woman belonged to a sphere lower than human. But in this century, which is the century of light and the revelation of mysteries, God is proving to the satisfaction of humanity that all this is ignorance and error, nay, rather, it is well established that mankind and womankind as parts of composite humanity are coequal and that no difference in estimate is allowable, for all are human. The conditions in past centuries were due to woman's lack of opportunity. She was denied the right and privilege of education and left in her undeveloped state. Naturally, she could not and did not advance. In reality, God has created all mankind, and in the estimation of God there is no distinction as to male and female. The one whose heart is pure is acceptable in His sight, be that one man or woman. God does not inquire, ''Art thou woman or art thou man?'' He judges human actions. If these are acceptable in the threshold of the Glorious One, man and woman will be equally recognized and rewarded.

(The Promulgation of Universal Peace, 1982 U.S. edition, p. 133)

16. The world of humanity consists of two parts: male and female. Each is the complement of the other. Therefore, if one is defective, the other will necessarily be incomplete, and perfection cannot be attained. There is a right hand and a left hand in the human body, functionally equal in service and administration. If either proves defective, the defect will naturally extend to the other by involving the completeness of the whole; for accomplishment is not normal unless both are perfect. If we say one hand is deficient, we prove the inability and incapacity of the other; for single-handed there is no full accomplishment. Just as physical accomplishment is complete with two hands, so man and woman, the two parts of the social body, must be perfect. It is not natural that either should remain undeveloped; and until both are perfected, the happiness of the human world will not be realized.

(*The Promulgation of Universal Peace*, 1982
U.S. edition, p. 134)

17. The status of woman in former times was exceedingly deplorable, for it was the belief of the Orient that it was best for woman to be ignorant. It was considered preferable that she should not know reading or writing in order that she might not be informed of events in the world. Woman was considered to be created for rearing children and attending to the duties of the household. If she pursued educational courses, it was deemed contrary to chastity; hence women were made prisoners of the household. The houses did not even have windows opening upon the outside world. Bahá'u'lláh destroyed these ideas and proclaimed the equality of man and woman. He made woman respected by commanding that all women be educated, that there be no difference in the education of the two sexes and that man and woman share the same rights. In the estimation of God there is no distinction of sex. One whose thought is pure, whose education is superior, whose scientific attainments are greater, whose deeds of philanthropy excel, be that one man or woman, white or coloured, is entitled to full rights and recognition; there is no differentiation whatsoever.

(*The Promulgation of Universal Peace*, 1982
U.S. edition, p. 166)

18. Woman's lack of progress and proficiency has been due to her need of equal education and opportunity. Had she been allowed this equality, there is no doubt she would be the counterpart of man in

ability and capacity. The happiness of mankind will be realized when women and men coordinate and advance equally, for each is the complement and helpmeet of the other.
(The Promulgation of Universal Peace, 1982 U.S. edition, p. 182)

19. He establishes the equality of man and woman. This is peculiar to the teachings of Bahá'u'lláh, for all other religions have placed man above woman.
(The Promulgation of Universal Peace, 1982 U.S. edition, p. 455)

20. Women have equal rights with men upon earth; in religion and society they are a very important element. As long as women are prevented from attaining their highest possibilities, so long will men be unable to achieve the greatness which might be theirs.
(Paris Talks, 1961 U.K. edition, p. 133)

21. In the world of humanity . . . the female sex is treated as though inferior, and is not allowed equal rights and privileges. This condition is due not to nature, but to education. In the Divine Creation there is no such distinction. Neither sex is superior to the other in the sight of God. Why then should one sex assert the inferiority of the other, withholding just rights and privileges as though God had given His authority for such a course of action? If women received the same educational advantages as those of men, the result would demonstrate the equality of capacity of both for scholarship.
   In some respects woman is superior to man. She is more tender-hearted, more receptive, her intuition is more intense.
(Paris Talks, 1961 U.K. edition, p. 161)

22. Divine Justice demands that the rights of both sexes should be equally respected since neither is superior to the other in the eyes of Heaven. Dignity before God depends, not on sex, but on purity and luminosity of heart. Human virtues belong equally to all!
(Paris Talks, 1961 U.K. edition, p. 162)

23. In this Revelation of Bahá'u'lláh, the women go neck and neck with the men. In no movement will they be left behind. Their rights with men are equal in degree. They will enter all the administrative branches of politics. They will attain in all such a degree as will be

11

considered the very highest station of the world of humanity and will take part in all affairs. Rest ye assured. Do ye not look upon the present conditions; in the not far distant future the world of women will become all-refulgent and all-glorious, *For His Holiness Bahá'u'lláh Hath Willed It so!* At the time of elections the right to vote is the inalienable right of women, and the entrance of women into all human departments is an irrefutable and incontrovertible question. No soul can retard or prevent it.

But there are certain matters, the participation in which is not worthy of women. For example, at the time when the community is taking up vigorous defensive measures against the attack of foes, the women are exempt from military engagements. It may so happen that at a given time warlike and savage tribes may furiously attack the body politic with the intention of carrying on a wholesale slaughter of its members; under such a circumstance defence is necessary, but it is the duty of men to organize and execute such defensive measures and not the women—because their hearts are tender and they cannot endure the sight of the horror of carnage, even if it is for the sake of defence. From such and similar undertakings the women are exempt.

As regards the constitution of the House of Justice, Bahá'u'lláh addresses the men. He says: "O ye men of the House of Justice!"

But when its members are to be elected, the right which belongs to women, so far as their voting and their voice is concerned, is indisputable. When the women attain to the ultimate degree of progress, then, according to the exigency of the time and place and their great capacity, they shall obtain extraordinary privileges. Be ye confident on these accounts. His Holiness Bahá'u'lláh has greatly strengthened the cause of women, and the rights and privileges of women is one of the greatest principles of 'Abdu'l-Bahá. Rest ye assured! Ere long the days shall come when the men addressing the women, shall say: *"Blessed are ye! Blessed are ye! Verily ye are worthy of every gift. Verily ye deserve to adorn your heads with the crown of everlasting glory, because in sciences and arts, in virtues and perfections ye shall become equal to man, and as regards tenderness of heart and the abundance of mercy and sympathy ye are superior".*
(*Paris Talks*, 1961 U.K. edition, pp. 182–184)

24. The woman of the East has progressed. Formerly in India, Persia and throughout the Orient, she was not considered a human being. Certain Arab tribes counted their women in with the live stock. In

their language the noun for woman also meant donkey; that is, the same name applied to both and a man's wealth was accounted by the number of these beasts of burden he possessed. The worst insult one could hurl at a man was to cry out, "Thou woman!" From the moment Bahá'u'lláh appeared, this changed. He did away with the idea of distinction between the sexes, proclaiming them equal in every capacity.

In former times it was considered wiser that woman should not know how to read or write; she should occupy herself only with drudgery. She was very ignorant. Bahá'u'lláh declares the education of woman to be of more importance than that of man. If the mother be ignorant, even if the father have great knowledge, the child's education will be at fault, for education begins with the milk. A child at the breast is like a tender branch that the gardener can train as he wills.

The East has begun to educate its women. Some there are in Persia who have become liberated through this cause, whose cleverness and eloquence the 'ulamá cannot refute. Many of them are poets. They are absolutely fearless. . . .

I hope for a like degree of progress among the women of Europe—that each may shine like unto a lamp; that they may cry out the proclamation of the kingdom; that they may truly assist the men; nay, that they may be even superior to the men, versed in sciences and yet detached, so that the whole world may bear witness to the fact that men and women have absolutely the same rights. It would be a cause of great joy for me to see such women. This is useful work; by it woman will enter into the kingdom. Otherwise, there will be no results.   ('Abdu'l-Bahá on Divine Philosophy,
1917 edition, pp. 81–83)

25. The world in the past has been ruled by force, and man has dominated over woman by reason of his more forceful and aggressive qualities both of body and mind. But the balance is already shifting—force is losing its weight and mental alertness, intuition, and the spiritual qualities of love and service, in which woman is strong, are gaining ascendancy. Hence the new age will be an age less masculine, and more permeated with the feminine ideals—or, to speak more exactly, will be an age in which the masculine and feminine elements of civilization will be more evenly balanced.
(Bahá'u'lláh and the New Era, 1976 U.S. edition,
p. 156)

Extracts from Letters Written by the Universal House of Justice:

26. If presented properly the position of women in the Bahá'í teachings will surely attract much attention, for it is not only legal but also spiritual and educational. Our ideals are so high and at the same time so practicable that all other views will fall short if compared to them.

(7 January 1931 to a National Spiritual Assembly)

27. As regards your question concerning the membership of the Universal House of Justice, there is a Tablet from 'Abdu'l-Bahá in which he definitely states that the membership of the Universal House of Justice is confined to men, and that the wisdom of it will be fully revealed and appreciated in the future. In the local, as well as the national Houses of Justice, however, women have the full right of membership. It is, therefore, only to the International House that they cannot be elected. The Bahá'ís should accept this statement of the Master in a spirit of deep faith, confident that there is a divine guidance and wisdom behind it which will be gradually unfolded to the eyes of the world.

(28 July 1936 to an individual believer)

28. As regards the membership of the International House of Justice, 'Abdu'l-Bahá states in a Tablet that it is confined to men, and that the wisdom of it will be revealed as manifest as the sun in the future. In any case the believers should know that, as 'Abdu'l-Bahá Himself has explicitly stated that sexes are equal except in some cases, the exclusion of women from the International House of Justice should not be surprising. From the fact that there is no equality of functions between the sexes one should not, however, infer that either sex is inherently superior or inferior to the other, or that they are unequal in their rights.

(14 December 1940 to a National Spiritual Assembly)

29. It is apparent from the Guardian's writings that where Bahá'u'lláh has expressed a law as between a man and a woman it applies, *mutatis mutandis*, between a woman and a man unless the context should make this impossible. For example the text of the Kitáb-i-Aqdas forbids a man to marry his father's wife (i.e. his step-mother) and the Guardian has indicated that likewise a woman is forbidden to marry her step-father.
(28 April 1974 to an individual believer)

30. Concerning your questions about the equality of men and women, this, as 'Abdu'l-Bahá has often explained, is a fundamental principle of Bahá'u'lláh, therefore the Laws of the Aqdas should be studied in the light of it. Equality between men and women does not, indeed physiologically it cannot, mean identity of functions. In some things women excel men, for others men are better fitted than women, while in very many things the difference of sex is of no effect at all. The differences of function are most apparent in family life. The capacity for motherhood has many far-reaching implications which are recognized in Bahá'í Law. For example, when it is not possible to educate all one's children, daughters receive preference over sons as mothers are the first educators of the next generation. Again, for physiological reasons, women are granted certain exemptions from fasting that are not applicable to men.
(24 July 1975 to an individual believer)

31. The primary question to be resolved is how the present world, with its entrenched pattern of conflict, can change to a world in which harmony and co-operation will prevail.

World order can be founded only on an unshakeable consciousness of the oneness of mankind, a spiritual truth which all the human sciences confirm. Anthropology, physiology, psychology, recognize only one human species, albeit infinitely varied in the secondary aspects of life. Recognition of this truth requires abandonment of prejudice—prejudice of every kind—race, class, colour, creed, nation, sex, degree of material civilization, everything which enables people to consider themselves superior to others.

Acceptance of the oneness of mankind is the first fundamental prerequisite for reorganization and administration of the world as one country, the home of humankind. Universal acceptance of this spiritual principle is essential to any successful attempt to establish world peace.   (October 1985)

Extracts from Letters Written on Behalf of the Universal House of Justice:

32. To the general premise that women and men have equality in the Faith, this, as often explained by 'Abdu'l-Bahá, is a fundamental principle deriving from Bahá'u'lláh and therefore His mention of the "Men of Justice" in the Kitáb-i-Aqdas should be considered in light of that principle.
(29 June 1976 to an individual believer)

33. 'Abdu'l-Bahá asserts: "In this divine age the bounties of God have encompassed the world of women. Equality of men and women, except in some negligible instances, has been fully and categorically announced. Distinctions have been utterly removed." That men and women differ from one another in certain characteristics and functions is an inescapable fact of nature; the important thing is that He regards such inequalities as remain between the sexes as being "negligible".
(8 January 1981 to a National Spiritual Assembly)

34. You are quite right in stating that men and women have basic and distinct qualities. The solution provided in the teachings of Bahá'u'lláh is not, as you correctly observe, for men to become women, and for women to become men. 'Abdu'l-Bahá gave us the key to the problem when He taught that the qualities and functions of men and women "complement" each other. He further elucidated this point when He said that the "new age" will be "an age in which the masculine and feminine elements of civilization will be more properly balanced."
(22 April 1981 to an individual believer)

35. It may be helpful to stress . . . that the Bahá'í principle of the equality of men and women is clearly stated in the teachings, and the fact that there is diversity of function between them in certain areas does not negate this principle.
(23 August 1984 to an individual believer)

II
The Role of Education in the Development of Women

Extracts from the Writings and Utterances of Bahá'u'lláh:

36. It is the bounden duty of parents to rear their children to be staunch in faith, . . . for every praiseworthy deed is born out of the light of religion, and lacking this supreme bestowal the child will not turn away from any evil, nor will he draw nigh unto any good.

(Bahá'í Education, A Compilation, 1976 World Centre edition, p. 6)

Extracts from the Writings and Utterances of 'Abdu'l-Bahá:

37. Praised be God, the women believers have organized meetings where they will learn how to teach the Faith, will spread the sweet savours of the Teachings and make plans for training the children.
. . . those present should concern themselves with every means of training the girl children; with teaching the various branches of knowledge, good behaviour, a proper way of life, the cultivation of a good character, chastity and constancy, perseverance, strength, determination, firmness of purpose; with household management, the education of children, and whatever especially applieth to the needs of girls—to the end that these girls, reared in the stronghold of all perfections, and with the protection of a goodly character, will, when they themselves become mothers, bring up their children from earliest infancy to have a good character and conduct themselves well.

Let them also study whatever will nurture the health of the body and its physical soundness, and how to guard their children from disease.

(Selections from the Writings of 'Abdu'l-Bahá, 1978 World Centre edition, pp. 123–124)

38. Work ye for the guidance of the women in that land, teach the young girls and the children, so that the mothers may educate their little ones from their earliest days, thoroughly train them, rear them to have a goodly character and good morals, guide them to all the virtues of humankind, prevent the development of any behaviour that would be worthy of blame, and foster them in the embrace of Bahá'í education. Thus shall these tender infants be nurtured at the breast of the knowledge of God and His love. Thus shall they grow and flourish, and be taught righteousness and the dignity of humankind, resolution and the will to strive and to endure. Thus shall they learn perseverance in all things, the will to advance, high mindedness and high resolve, chastity and purity of life. Thus shall they be enabled to carry to a successful conclusion whatsoever they undertake.

Let the mothers consider that whatever concerneth the education of children is of the first importance. Let them put forth every effort in this regard, for when the bough is green and tender it will grow in whatever way ye train it. Therefore it is incumbent upon the mothers to rear their little ones even as a gardener tendeth his young plants. Let them strive by day and by night to establish within their children faith and certitude, the fear of God, the love of the Beloved of the worlds, and all good qualities and traits. Whensoever a mother seeth that her child hath done well, let her praise and applaud him and cheer his heart; and if the slightest undesirable trait should manifest itself, let her counsel the child and punish him, and use means based on reason, even a slight verbal chastisement should this be necessary. It is not, however, permissible to strike a child, or vilify him, for the child's character will be totally perverted if he be subjected to blows or verbal abuse.

> *(Selections from the Writings of 'Abdu'l-Bahá, 1978 World Centre edition, pp. 124–125)*

39. . . . it is incumbent upon the father and mother to train their children both in good conduct and the study of books; study, that is, to the degree required, so that no child, whether girl or boy, will remain illiterate.

> *(Selections from the Writings of 'Abdu'l-Bahá, 1978 World Centre edition, p. 127)*

40. 'Abdu'l-Bahá's supreme joy is in observing that a number of leaves from among the handmaidens of the Blessed Beauty have been educated, that they are the essence of detachment, and are well-

informed of the mysteries of the world of being; that they raise such a call in their glorification and praise of the Greatest Name as to cause the inmates of the Fanes of the Kingdom to become attracted and overjoyed, and that they recite prayers in prose and poetry, and melodiously chant the divine verses. I cherish the hope that thou wilt be one of them, wilt cast forth pearls, wilt be constantly engaged in singing His praise and wilt intone celestial strains in glorification of His attributes.

(Extract from previously untranslated Tablet)

41. O esteemed handmaid! . . . Thou hast written about the girls' school. What was previously written still holdeth true. There can be no improvement unless the girls are brought up in schools and centres of learning, unless they are taught the sciences and other branches of knowledge, and unless they acquire the manifold arts, as necessary, and are divinely trained. For the day will come when these girls will become mothers. Mothers are the first educators of children, who establish virtues in the child's inner nature. They encourage the child to acquire perfections and goodly manners, warn him against unbecoming qualities, and encourage him to show forth resolve, firmness, and endurance under hardship, and to advance on the highroad to progress. Due regard for the education of girls is, therefore, necessary. This is a very important subject, and it should be administered and organized under the aegis of the Spiritual Assembly.

(Extract from previously untranslated Tablet)

42. . . . it is incumbent upon the girls of this glorious era to be fully versed in the various branches of knowledge, in sciences and the arts and all the wonders of this pre-eminent time, that they may then educate their children and train them from their earliest days in the ways of perfection.

(Extract from previously untranslated Tablet)

43. Furthermore, the education of woman is more necessary and important than that of man, for woman is the trainer of the child from its infancy. If she be defective and imperfect herself, the child will necessarily be deficient; therefore, imperfection of woman implies a condition of imperfection in all mankind, for it is the mother who rears, nurtures and guides the growth of the child. This is not the function of the father. If the educator be incompetent, the educated

will be correspondingly lacking. This is evident and incontrovertible. Could the student be brilliant and accomplished if the teacher is illiterate and ignorant? The mothers are the first educators of mankind; if they be imperfect, alas for the condition and future of the race. . . .

It has been objected by some that woman is not equally capable with man and that she is deficient by creation. This is pure imagination. The difference in capability between man and woman is due entirely to opportunity and education. Heretofore woman has been denied the right and privilege of equal development. If equal opportunity be granted her, there is no doubt she would be the peer of man. History will evidence this. In past ages noted women have arisen in the affairs of nations and surpassed men in their accomplishments. . . .

The purpose, in brief, is this: that if woman be fully educated and granted her rights, she will attain the capacity for wonderful accomplishments and prove herself the equal of man. She is the coadjutor of man, his complement and helpmeet. Both are human; both are endowed with potentialities of intelligence and embody the virtues of humanity. In all human powers and functions they are partners and coequals. At present in spheres of human activity woman does not manifest her natal prerogatives, owing to lack of education and opportunity. Without doubt education will establish her equality with men.

(The Promulgation of Universal Peace, 1982 U.S. edition, pp. 133–137)

44. In proclaiming the oneness of mankind He taught that men and women are equal in the sight of God and that there is no distinction to be made between them. The only difference between them now is due to lack of education and training. If woman is given equal opportunity of education, distinction and estimate of inferiority will disappear. . . .

He promulgated the adoption of the same course of education for man and woman. Daughters and sons must follow the same curriculum of study, thereby promoting unity of the sexes. When all mankind shall receive the same opportunity of education and the equality of men and women be realized, the foundations of war will be utterly destroyed.

(The Promulgation of Universal Peace, 1982 U.S. edition, pp. 174–175)

21

45. Why should a woman be left mentally undeveloped? Science is praiseworthy—whether investigated by the intellect of man or woman. So, little by little, woman advanced, giving increasing evidence of equal capabilities with man—whether in scientific research, political ability or any other sphere of human activity. The conclusion is evident that woman has been outdistanced through lack of education and intellectual facilities. If given the same educational opportunities or course of study, she would develop the same capacity and abilities.

(*The Promulgation of Universal Peace*, 1982 U.S. edition, pp. 280–281)

46. Bahá'u'lláh has announced that inasmuch as ignorance and lack of education are barriers of separation among mankind, all must receive training and instruction. Through this provision the lack of mutual understanding will be remedied and the unity of mankind furthered and advanced. Universal education is a universal law. It is, therefore, incumbent upon every father to teach and instruct his children according to his possibilities. If he is unable to educate them, the body politic, the representative of the people, must provide the means for their education. . . .

The sex distinction which exists in the human world is due to the lack of education for woman, who has been denied equal opportunity for development and advancement. Equality of the sexes will be established in proportion to the increased opportunities afforded woman in this age, for man and woman are equally the recipients of powers and endowments from God, the Creator. God has not ordained distinction between them in His consummate purpose.

(*The Promulgation of Universal Peace*, 1982 U.S. edition, p. 300)

47. The education of each child is compulsory. . . . In addition to this widespread education each child must be taught a profession, art, or trade, so that every member of the community will be enabled to earn his own livelihood. Work done in the spirit of service is the highest form of worship.

(*Divine Philosophy*, 1917 edition, p. 78)

48. Devote ye particular attention to the school for girls, for the greatness of this wondrous Age will be manifested as a result of progress in the world of women. This is why ye observe that in every

land the world of women is on the march, and this is due to the impact of the Most Great Manifestation, and the power of the teachings of God.

(Bahá'í Education, a compilation, 1976 World Centre edition, p. 37)

49. O handmaid of the Most High! Our hearts rejoiced at thy letter concerning a school for girls.[5] Praised be God that there is now a school of this type in Ṭihrán where young maidens can, through His bounty, receive an education and with all vigour acquire the accomplishments of humankind. Ere long will women in every field keep pace with the men.

Until now, in Persia, the means for women's advancement were non-existent. But now, God be thanked, ever since the dawning of the Morn of Salvation, they have been going forward day by day. The hope is that they will take the lead in virtues and attainments, in closeness to the Court of Almighty God, in faith and certitude—and that the women of the East will become the envy of the women of the West.

(Bahá'í Education, a compilation, 1976 World Centre edition, p. 48)

Extract from a Letter Written by the Universal House of Justice:

50. The cause of universal education, which has already enlisted in its service an army of dedicated people from every faith and nation, deserves the utmost support that the governments of the world can lend it. For ignorance is indisputably the principal reason for the decline and fall of peoples and the perpetuation of prejudice. No nation can achieve success unless education is accorded all its citizens. Lack of resources limits the ability of many nations to fulfil this necessity, imposing a certain ordering of priorities. The decision-

---

5. The Tárbiyat School, Ṭihrán, Persia.

23

making agencies involved would do well to consider giving first priority to the education of women and girls, since it is through educated mothers that the benefits of knowledge can be most effectively and rapidly diffused throughout society. In keeping with the requirements of the times, consideration should also be given to teaching the concept of world citizenship as part of the standard education of every child.

(October 1985)

Extracts from Letters Written on Behalf of the Universal House of Justice:

51. A very important element in the attainment of such equality is Bahá'u'lláh's provision that boys and girls must follow essentially the same curriculum in schools.

(28 December 1980 to a National Spiritual Assembly)

52. The House of Justice regards the need to educate and guide women in their primary responsibility as mothers as an excellent opportunity for organizing women's activities. Your efforts should focus on helping them in their function as educators of the rising generation. Women should also be encouraged to attract their husbands and male members of their families to the Faith so that the Bahá'í community will be representative of the society of which it forms a part. Gradually the spirit of unity and fellowship, as set forth in our teachings, will be reflected in the life of Bahá'í families.

(29 February 1984 to a National Spiritual Assembly)

III.
Application of the Principle of Equality to Family Life

Extracts from the Writings of Bahá'u'lláh:

53. In the Name of God, the Peerless! O handmaid of God! Steadfastness in the Cause is mentioned in the Tablets and set forth by the Pen of the Ancient of Days. Render thanks to the Beloved of the world that thou hast set thy heart on Him and art uttering His praise. Many a man hath in this day been deprived of making mention of the All-Sufficing Lord and of recognizing His truth; and many a woman hath fixed her gaze upon the Horizon of the Most High, and hath adorned herself with the garb of the love of the Desire of the world. This is God's grace which He bestoweth upon whomsoever He pleaseth. By the Daystar of ancient mysteries! The sweet-scented fragrance of every breath breathed in the love of God is wafted in the court of the presence of the Lord of Revelation. The reward of no good deed is or ever will be lost. Blessed art thou, doubly blessed art thou! Thou art reckoned amongst those handmaidens whose love for their kin hath not prevented them from attaining the shores of the Sea of Grace and Mercy. God willing, thou shalt rest eternally neath the shade of the favours of the All-Merciful and shalt be assured of His bounties. Engage in the praise of the True One and rejoice in His loving kindness.

The world passeth away, and that which is everlasting is the love of God. God willing, thou shalt circumambulate the True One in every world of His worlds and shalt be free from all else save Him.
(Extract from previously untranslated Tablet)

54. All should know, and in this regard attain the splendours of the sun of certitude, and be illumined thereby: Women and men have been and will always be equal in the sight of God. The Dawning-Place of the Light of God sheddeth its radiance upon all with the same effulgence. Verily God created women for men, and men for women. The most beloved of people before God are the most steadfast and those who have surpassed others in their love for God, exalted be His glory.

The friends of God must be adorned with the ornament of justice, equity, kindness and love. As they do not allow themselves to be the object of cruelty and transgression, in like manner they should not allow such tyranny to visit the handmaidens of God. He, verily, speaketh the truth and commandeth that which benefitteth His servants and handmaidens. He is the Protector of all in this world and the next.

(Extract from previously untranslated Tablet)

Extracts from the Writings and Utterances of 'Abdu'l-Bahá:

55. O ye two believers in God! The Lord, peerless is He, hath made woman and man to abide with each other in the closest companionship, and to be even as a single soul. They are two helpmates, two intimate friends, who should be concerned about the welfare of each other.

If they live thus, they will pass through this world with perfect contentment, bliss, and peace of heart, and become the object of divine grace and favour in the Kingdom of heaven. But if they do other than this, they will live out their lives in great bitterness, longing at every moment for death, and will be shamefaced in the heavenly realm.

Strive, then, to abide, heart and soul, with each other as two doves in the nest, for this is to be blessed in both worlds.

(*Selections from the Writings of 'Abdu'l-Bahá*, 1978 World Centre edition, p. 122)

56. . . . following the precepts of God and the holy Law, suckle your children from their infancy with the milk of a universal education, and rear them so that from their earliest days, within their inmost heart, their very nature, a way of life will be firmly established that will conform to the divine Teachings in all things.

For mothers are the first educators, the first mentors; and truly it is the mothers who determine the happiness, the future greatness, the courteous ways and learning and judgement, the understanding and the faith of their little ones.

(Selections from the Writings of 'Abdu'l-Bahá,
1978 World Centre edition, p. 126)

57. . . . it is enjoined upon the father and mother, as a duty, to strive with all effort to train the daughter and the son, to nurse them from the breast of knowledge and to rear them in the bosom of sciences and arts. Should they neglect this matter, they shall be held responsible and worthy of reproach in the presence of the stern Lord.

(Selections from the Writings of 'Abdu'l-Bahá,
1978 World Centre edition, p. 127)

58. O ye loving mothers, know ye that in God's sight, the best of all ways to worship Him is to educate the children and train them in all the perfections of humankind; and no nobler deed than this can be imagined.

(Selections from the Writings of 'Abdu'l-Bahá,
1978 World Centre edition, p. 139)

59. Note ye how easily, where unity existeth in a given family, the affairs of that family are conducted; what progress the members of that family make, how they prosper in the world. Their concerns are in order, they enjoy comfort and tranquillity, they are secure, their position is assured, they come to be envied by all. Such a family but addeth to its stature and its lasting honour, as day succeedeth day.

(Selections from the Writings of 'Abdu'l-Bahá,
1978 World Centre edition, p. 279)

60. You have asked whether a husband would be able to prevent his wife from embracing the divine light or a wife dissuade her husband from gaining entry into the Kingdom of God. In truth neither of them could prevent the other from entering into the Kingdom, unless the husband hath an excessive attachment to the wife or the wife to the husband. Indeed when either of the two worshippeth the other to the exclusion of God, then each could prevent the other from seeking admittance into His Kingdom.

(Family Life, 1982 U.K. Publishing Trust, p. 8)

61. *Question*: What is the attitude of your belief toward the family?

Answer: According to the teachings of Bahá'u'lláh the family, being a human unit, must be educated according to the rules of sanctity. All the virtues must be taught the family. The integrity of the family bond must be constantly considered, and the rights of the individual members must not be transgressed. The rights of the son, the father, the mother—none of them must be transgressed, none of them must be arbitrary. Just as the son has certain obligations to his father, the father, likewise, has certain obligations to his son. The mother, the sister and other members of the household have their certain prerogatives. All these rights and prerogatives must be conserved, yet the unity of the family must be sustained. The injury of one shall be considered the injury of all; the comfort of each, the comfort of all; the honour of one, the honour of all.

> (*The Promulgation of Universal Peace*, 1982 U.S. edition, p. 168)

Extracts from Letters Written on Behalf of the Guardian to Individual Believers (unless otherwise cited):

62. When such difference of opinion and belief occurs between husband and wife it is very unfortunate for undoubtedly it detracts from that spiritual bond which is the stronghold of the family bond, especially in times of difficulty. The way, however, that it could be remedied is not by acting in such wise as to alienate the other party. One of the objects of the Cause is actually to bring about a closer bond in the homes. In all such cases, therefore, the Master used to advise obedience to the wishes of the other party and prayer. Pray that your husband may gradually see the light and at the same time so act as to draw him nearer rather than prejudice him. Once that harmony is secured then you will be able to serve unhampered.

> (15 July 1928)

63. Shoghi Effendi trusts that as a result of his cable and this letter

your wife will be able to devote a little more time to her family, but he also hopes that you will be able to assist her in obtaining the time and opportunity to serve a Cause that is so dear and near to her heart and in which her services are much appreciated.
(19 June 1931)

64. The Guardian, in his remarks . . . about parents' and children's, wives' and husbands' relations in America, meant that there is a tendency in that country for children to be too independent of the wishes of their parents and lacking in the respect due to them. Also wives, in some cases, have a tendency to exert an unjust degree of domination over their husbands which, of course, is not right, any more than that the husband should unjustly dominate his wife.
(22 July 1943)

65. It is one of the essential teachings of the Faith that unity should be maintained in the home. Of course this does not mean that any member of the family has a right to influence the faith of any other member; and if this is realized by all the members, then it seems certain that unity would be feasible.
(6 July 1952)

66. The Guardian fully appreciates your desire to go forth as a pioneer at this time, and to help establish the Faith in the virgin areas; but you should not go against the wishes of your husband, and force him to give up everything in order that you might serve the Faith in this manner. We must bear in mind the wishes and the rights of those who are closely connected in our lives.

If your husband wishes you to remain where you are, certainly there is a vast field for teaching there.
(31 July 1953)

67. Wherever there is a Bahá'í family, those concerned should by all means do all they can to preserve it, because divorce is strongly condemned in the Teachings, whereas harmony, unity and love are held up as the highest ideals in human relationships. This must always apply to the Bahá'ís, whether they are serving in the pioneering field or not.
(9 November 1956)

Extracts from Letters Written on Behalf of the Universal House of Justice to Individual Believers (unless otherwise cited):

68. That the first teacher of the child is the mother should not be startling, for the primary orientation of the infant is to its mother. This provision of nature in no way minimizes the role of the father in the Bahá'í family. Again, equality of status does not mean identity of function.

(23 June 1974)

69. In considering the problems that you and your wife are experiencing, the House of Justice points out that the unity of your family should take priority over any other consideration. Bahá'u'lláh came to bring unity to the world, and a fundamental unity is that of the family. Therefore, we must believe that the Faith is intended to strengthen the family, not weaken it. For example, service to the Cause should not produce neglect of the family. It is important for you to arrange your time so that your family life is harmonious and your household receives the attention it requires.

Bahá'u'lláh also stressed the importance of consultation. We should not think this worthwhile method of seeking solutions is confined to the administrative institutions of the Cause. Family consultation employing full and frank discussion, and animated by awareness of the need for moderation and balance, can be the panacea for domestic conflict. Wives should not attempt to dominate their husbands, nor husbands their wives.

(1 August 1978)

70. Noting that you and your husband have consulted about your family problems with your Spiritual Assembly but did not receive any advice, and also discussed your situation with a family counsellor without success, the House of Justice feels it most essential for your husband and you to understand that marriage can be a source of well-being, conveying a sense of security and spiritual happiness.

However, it is not something that just happens. For marriage to become a haven of contentment it requires the cooperation of the marriage partners themselves, and the assistance of their families. (24 June 1979)

71. The members of a family all have duties and responsibilities towards one another and to the family as a whole, and these duties and responsibilities vary from member to member because of their natural relationships. The parents have the inescapable duty to educate their children—but not vice versa; the children have the duty to obey their parents—the parents do not obey the children; the mother—not the father—bears the children, nurses them in babyhood, and is thus their first educator, hence daughters have a prior right to education over sons and, as the Guardian's secretary has written on his behalf, "The task of bringing up a Bahá'í child, as emphasized time and again in Bahá'í Writings, is the chief responsibility of the mother, whose unique privilege is indeed to create in her home such conditions as would be most conducive to both his material and spiritual welfare and advancement. The training which a child first receives through his mother constitutes the strongest foundation for his future development." A corollary of this responsibility of the mother is her right to be supported by her husband—a husband has no explicit right to be supported by his wife. . . .

In any group, however loving the consultation, there are nevertheless points on which, from time to time, agreement cannot be reached. In a Spiritual Assembly this dilemma is resolved by a majority vote. There can, however, be no majority where only two parties are involved, as in the case of a husband and wife. There are, therefore, times when a wife should defer to her husband, and times when a husband should defer to his wife, but neither should ever unjustly dominate the other. In short, the relationship between husband and wife should be as held forth in the prayer revealed by 'Abdu'l-Bahá which is often read at Bahá'í weddings: "Verily, they are married in obedience to Thy command. Cause them to become the signs of harmony and unity until the end of time."

These are all relationships within the family, but there is a much wider sphere of relationships between men and women than in the home, and this too we should consider in the context of Bahá'í society, not in that of past or present social norms. For example, although the mother is the first educator of the child, and the most important formative influence in his development, the father also has the

32

responsibility of educating his children, and this responsibility is so weighty that Bahá'u'lláh has stated that a father who fails to exercise it forfeits his rights of fatherhood. Similarly, although the primary responsibility for supporting the family financially is placed upon the husband, this does not by any means imply that the place of women is confined to the home.

(23 December 1980 to a National Spiritual Assembly)

72. You have asked, however, for specific rules of conduct to govern the relationships of husbands and wives. This the House of Justice does not wish to do, and it feels that there is already adequate guidance included in the compilation on this subject. For example the principle that the rights of each and all in the family unit must be upheld, and the advice that loving consultation should be the keynote, that all matters should be settled in harmony and love, and that there are times when the husband and the wife should defer to the wishes of the other. Exactly under what circumstances such deference should take place, is a matter for each couple to determine.

(16 May 1982)

73. You ask about the admonition that everyone must work, and want to know if this means that you, a wife and mother, must work for a livelihood as your husband does. We are requested to enclose for your perusal an excerpt, "The twelfth Glad-Tidings", from Bahá'u'lláh's "Tablet of Bishárát."[6] You will see that the directive is for the friends to be engaged in an occupation which will be of benefit to mankind. Homemaking is a highly honourable and responsible work of fundamental importance for mankind.

(16 June 1982)

74. With regard to your question whether mothers should work outside the home, it is helpful to consider the matter from the perspective of the concept of a Bahá'í family. This concept is based on the principle that the man has primary responsibility for the financial support of the family, and the woman is the chief and primary educator of the children. This by no means implies that these functions are inflexibly fixed and cannot be changed and adjusted to suit particular family situations, nor does it mean that the place of the woman is con-

---

6. This passage appears in the present compilation, see No. 76.

fined to the home. Rather, while primary responsibility is assigned, it is anticipated that fathers would play a significant role in the education of the children and women could also be breadwinners. As you rightly indicated, 'Abdu'l-Bahá encouraged women to "participate fully and equally in the affairs of the world".

In relation to your specific queries, the decision concerning the amount of time a mother may spend in working outside the home depends on circumstances existing within the home, which may vary from time to time. Family consultation will help to provide the answers.
                    (9 August 1984)

75. The great importance attached to the mother's role derives from the fact that she is the *first* educator of the child. Her attitude, her prayers, even what she eats and her physical condition have a great influence on the child when it is still in the womb. When the child is born, it is she who has been endowed by God with the milk which is the first food designed for it, and it is intended that, if possible, she should be with the baby to train and nurture it in its earliest days and months. This does not mean that the father does not also love, pray for, and care for his baby, but as he has the primary responsibility of providing for the family, his time to be with his child is usually limited, while the mother is usually closely associated with the baby during this intensely formative time when it is growing and developing faster than it ever will again during the whole of its life. As the child grows older and more independent, the relative nature of its relationship with its mother and father modifies and the father can play a greater role.
                    (23 August 1984)

34

IV.
Women in the World at Large

Extract from the Writings of Bahá'u'lláh:

76. It is enjoined upon every one of you to engage in some form of occupation, such as crafts, trades and the like. We have graciously exalted your engagement in such work to the rank of worship unto God, the True One. Ponder ye in your hearts the grace and the blessings of God and render thanks unto Him at eventide and at dawn. Waste not your time in idleness and sloth. Occupy yourselves with that which profiteth yourselves and others. Thus hath it been decreed in this Tablet from whose horizon the day-star of wisdom and utterance shineth resplendent.

The most despised of men in the sight of God are those who sit idly and beg. Hold ye fast unto the cord of material means, placing your whole trust in God, the Provider of all means. When anyone occupieth himself in a craft or trade, such occupation itself is regarded in the estimation of God as an act of worship; and this is naught but a token of His infinite and all-pervasive bounty.

> (*Tablets of Bahá'u'lláh revealed after the Kitáb-i-Aqdas*, 1978 World Centre edition, p. 26)

Extracts from the Writings and Utterances of 'Abdu'l-Bahá:

77. The handmaidens of God and the bondsmaids in His divine Court should reveal such attributes and attitudes amongst the women of the world as would cause them to stand out and achieve renown in the circles of women. That is, they should associate with them with supreme chastity and steadfast decency, with unshakeable faith, ar-

ticulate speech, an eloquent tongue, irrefutable testimony and high resolve. Beseech God that thou mayest attain unto all these bounties. (Extract from previously untranslated Tablet)

78. Until the reality of equality between man and woman is fully established and attained, the highest social development of mankind is not possible. Even granted that woman is inferior to man in some degree of capacity or accomplishment, this or any other distinction would continue to be productive of discord and trouble. The only remedy is education, opportunity; for equality means equal qualification. . . .
  And let it be known once more that until woman and man recognize and realize equality, social and political progress here or anywhere will not be possible.
  (The Promulgation of Universal Peace, 1982 U.S. edition, pp. 76–77)

79. . . . the principle of religion has been revealed by Bahá'u'lláh that woman must be given the privilege of equal education with man and full right to his prerogatives. That is to say, there must be no difference in the education of male and female in order that womankind may develop equal capacity and importance with man in the social and economic equation. Then the world will attain unity and harmony. In past ages humanity has been defective and inefficient because it has been incomplete. War and its ravages have blighted the world; the education of woman will be a mighty step toward its abolition and ending, for she will use her whole influence against war. Woman rears the child and educates the youth to maturity. She will refuse to give her sons for sacrifice upon the field of battle. In truth, she will be the greatest factor in establishing universal peace and international arbitration. Assuredly, woman will abolish warfare among mankind.
  (The Promulgation of Universal Peace, 1982 U.S. edition, p. 108)

80. Again, it is well established in history that where woman has not participated in human affairs the outcomes have never attained a state of completion and perfection. On the other hand, every influential undertaking of the human world wherein woman has been a participant has attained importance. This is historically true and beyond disproof even in religion. Jesus Christ had twelve disciples and

among His followers a woman known as Mary Magdalene. Judas Iscariot had become a traitor and hypocrite, and after the crucifixion the remaining eleven disciples were wavering and undecided. It is certain from the evidence of the Gospels that the one who comforted them and reestablished their faith was Mary Magdalene. . . . The most momentous question of this day is international peace and arbitration, and universal peace is impossible without universal suffrage. (*The Promulgation of Universal Peace*, 1982 U.S. edition, pp. 134–135)

81. *Question:* Is it not a fact that universal peace cannot be accomplished until there is political democracy in all the countries of the world?

Answer: It is very evident that in the future there shall be no centralization in the countries of the world, be they constitutional in government, republican or democratic in form. The United States may be held up as the example of future government—that is to say, each province will be independent in itself, but there will be federal union protecting the interests of the various independent states. It may not be a republican or a democratic form. To cast aside centralization which promotes despotism is the exigency of the time. This will be productive of international peace. Another fact of equal importance in bringing about international peace is woman's suffrage. That is to say, when perfect equality shall be established between men and women, peace may be realized for the simple reason that womankind in general will never favour warfare. Women will not be willing to allow those whom they have so tenderly cared for to go to the battlefield. When they shall have a vote, they will oppose any cause of warfare. Another factor which will bring about universal peace is the linking together of the Orient and the Occident. (*The Promulgation of Universal Peace*, 1982 U.S. edition, p. 167)

82. When all mankind shall receive the same opportunity of education and the equality of men and women be realized, the foundations of war will be utterly destroyed. Without equality this will be impossible because all differences and distinction are conducive to discord and strife. Equality between men and women is conducive to the abolition of warfare for the reason that women will never be willing to sanction it. (*The Promulgation of Universal Peace*, 1982 U.S. edition, p. 175)

38

83. Woman must especially devote her energies and abilities toward the industrial and agricultural sciences, seeking to assist mankind in that which is most needful. By this means she will demonstrate capability and ensure recognition of equality in the social and economic equation.

(*The Promulgation of Universal Peace*, 1982
U.S. edition, p. 283)

84. Therefore, strive to show in the human world that women are most capable and efficient, that their hearts are more tender and susceptible than the hearts of men, that they are more philanthropic and responsive toward the needy and suffering, that they are inflexibly opposed to war and are lovers of peace. Strive that the ideal of international peace may become realized through the efforts of womankind, for man is more inclined to war than woman, and a real evidence of woman's superiority will be her service and efficiency in the establishment of universal peace.

(*The Promulgation of Universal Peace*, 1982
U.S. edition, p. 284)

85. . . . imbued with the same virtues as man, rising through all the degrees of human attainment, women will become the peers of men, and until this equality is established, true progress and attainment for the human race will not be facilitated.

The evident reasons underlying this are as follows: Woman by nature is opposed to war; she is an advocate of peace. Children are reared and brought up by the mothers who give them the first principles of education and labour assiduously in their behalf. Consider, for instance, a mother who has tenderly reared a son for twenty years to the age of maturity. Surely she will not consent to having that son torn asunder and killed in the field of battle. Therefore, as woman advances toward the degree of man in power and privilege, with the right of vote and control in human government, most assuredly war will cease; for woman is naturally the most devoted and staunch advocate of international peace.

(*The Promulgation of Universal Peace*, 1982
U.S. edition, p. 375)

86. According to the spirit of this age, women must advance and fulfill their mission in all departments of life, becoming equal to men. They must be on the same level as men and enjoy equal rights. This

is my earnest prayer and it is one of the fundamental principles of Bahá'u'lláh.

> (*Bahá'u'lláh and the New Era*, 1976 U.S. edition, p. 154)

87. The woman is indeed of the greater importance to the race. She has the greater burden and the greater work. Look at the vegetable and the animal worlds. The palm which carries the fruit is the tree most prized by the date grower. The Arab knows that for a long journey the mare has the longest wind. For her greater strength and fierceness, the lioness is more feared by the hunter than the lion. . . . The woman has greater moral courage than the man; she has also special gifts which enable her to govern in moments of danger and crisis.

> (*'Abdu'l-Bahá in London*, 1982 U.K. edition, pp. 102–103)

Extracts from Letters Written on Behalf of the Guardian:

88. Concerning Bahá'í representation at the All-Asian Women's Conference; this is undoubtedly a most commendable thing to do especially as the Cause has so much concerning the position of women in society. Shoghi Effendi hopes that the National Assembly will do its best to win the admiration of all the assembled delegates for the teachings of the Cause along that line. We should always take such opportunities that present themselves. Maybe we would succeed to render some service to society and alleviate its ills.

> (10 November 1930 to a National Spiritual Assembly)

89. What 'Abdu'l-Bahá meant about the women arising for peace is that this is a matter which vitally affects women, and when they form a conscious and overwhelming mass of public opinion against war

there can be no war. The Bahá'í women are already organized through being members of the Faith and the Administrative Order. No further organization is needed. But they should, through teaching and through the active moral support they give to every movement directed towards peace, seek to exert a strong influence on other women's minds in regard to this essential matter.

(24 March 1945 to an individual believer)

Extract from a Letter Written by the Universal House of Justice:

90. The emancipation of women, the achievement of full equality between the sexes, is one of the most important, though less acknowledged prerequisites of peace. The denial of such equality perpetrates an injustice against one half of the world's population and promotes in men harmful attitudes and habits that are carried from the family to the workplace, to political life, and ultimately to international relations. There are no grounds, moral, practical, or biological, upon which such denial can be justified. Only as women are welcomed into full partnership in all fields of human endeavour will the moral and psychological climate be created in which international peace can emerge.

(October 1985)

Extracts from Letters Written on Behalf of the Universal House of Justice:

91. . . . there is a much wider sphere of relationships between men and women than in the home, and this too we should consider in the

context of Bahá'í society, not in that of past or present social norms. For example, although the mother is the first educator of the child, and the most important formative influence in his development, the father also has the responsibility of educating his children, and this responsibility is so weighty that Bahá'u'lláh has stated that a father who fails to exercise it forfeits his rights of fatherhood. Similarly, although the primary responsibility for supporting the family financially is placed upon the husband, this does not by any means imply that the place of women is confined to the home. On the contrary, 'Abdu'l-Bahá has stated:

> "In this Revelation of Bahá'u'lláh, the women go neck and neck with the men. In no movement will they be left behind. Their rights with men are equal in degree. They will enter all the administrative branches of politics. They will attain in all such a degree as will be considered the very highest station of the world of humanity and will take part in all affairs."
> *(Paris Talks*, p. 182)

and again:

> "So it will come to pass that when women participate fully and equally in the affairs of the world, when they enter confidently and capably the great arena of laws and politics, war will cease;..."
> *(The Promulgation of Universal Peace*, p. 135)

In the Tablet to the World, Bahá'u'lláh Himself has envisaged that women as well as men would be breadwinners in stating:

> "Everyone, whether man or woman, should hand over to a trusted person a portion of what he or she earneth through trade, agriculture or other occupation, for the training and education of children, to be spent for this purpose with the knowledge of the Trustees of the House of Justice."
> *(Tablets of Bahá'u'lláh Revealed after the Kitáb-i-Aqdas*, p. 90)

> (28 December 1980 to a National Spiritual Assembly)

92. The duty of women in being the first educators of mankind is clearly set forth in the Writings. It is for every woman, if and when she becomes a mother, to determine how best she can discharge on

the one hand her chief responsibility as a mother and on the other, to the extent possible, to participate in other aspects of the activities of the society of which she forms a part.

(22 April 1981 to an individual believer)

V.
Fostering the Development of Women

Extracts from the Writings of Bahá'u'lláh:

93. He is the Light shining from the Horizon of Revelation! In this Day the Blessed Tree of Remembrance speaketh forth in the Kingdom of Utterance saying: Well is it with the servant who hath turned his face towards Him, and embraced His truth, and with the handmaiden who hath hearkened to His Voice and become of the blissful. Verily, she is a champion of the field of true understanding. To this the Tongue of Truth beareth witness from His exalted Station. O My leaf, blessed art thou for having responded to My call when it was raised in the name of the True One. Thou didst recognize My Revelation when men of renown were immersed in manifest idle fancies. Thou hast verily attained the mercy of thy Lord time and again. Render thanks unto Him and glorify Him with thy praise. He is, in truth, with His handmaidens and servants who have turned towards Him. The shining glory from the horizon of My Kingdom be upon thee and upon the one who hath guided thee to My straight path.
(Extract from previously untranslated Tablet)

94. We beseech the True One to adorn His handmaidens with the ornament of chastity, of trustworthiness, of righteousness and of purity. Verily, He is the All-Bestowing, the All-Generous. We make mention of the handmaidens of God at this time and announce unto them the glad-tidings of the tokens of the mercy and compassion of God and His consideration for them, glorified be He, and We supplicate Him for all His assistance to perform such deeds as are the cause of the exaltation of His Word. He verily speaketh the truth and enjoineth upon His servants and His handmaidens that which will profit them in every world of His worlds. He, verily, is the All-Forgiving, the All-Merciful.
(Extract from previously untranslated Tablet)

Extracts from the Writings and Utterances of 'Abdu'l-Bahá:

95. The effulgence of the rays of the Sun of Truth is abundant and the favours of the Blessed Beauty surround the women believers and the handmaidens who have attained unto certitude. At every moment a bounteous bestowal is revealed. The handmaidens of the Merciful should seize the opportunities afforded in these days. Each one should strive to draw nigh unto the divine Threshold and seek bounties from the Source of existence. She should attain such a state and be confirmed with such a power as to make, with but the utterance of one word, a lowly person to be held in reverence, initiate him who is deprived into the world of the spirit, impart hope to the despondent, endow the portionless one with a share of the great bestowal, and confer knowledge and insight upon the ignorant and the blind, and alertness and vigilance on the indolent and heedless. This is the attribute of the handmaidens of the Merciful. This is the characteristic of the bondsmaids of God's Threshold.

O ye leaves who have attained certitude! In the countries of Europe and America the maidservants of the Merciful have won the prize of excellence and advancement from the arena of men, and in the fields of teaching and spreading the divine fragrances they have shown a brilliant hand. Soon they will soar like the birds of the Concourse on high in the far corners of the world and will guide the people and reveal to them the divine mysteries. Ye, who are the blessed leaves from the East, should burn more brightly, and engage in spreading the sweet savours of the Lord and in reciting the verses of God. Arise, therefore, and exert yourselves to fulfil the exhortations and counsels of the Blessed Beauty, that all hopes may be realized and that the plain of streams and orchards may become the garden of oneness. Upon ye, men and women, be the glory of glories.

(Extract from previously untranslated Tablet)

96. In this great Cycle and wondrous Dispensation some women

47

have been raised up who were the emblems of unity and ensigns of oneness, for the revelation of divine bestowals is received by men and women in equal measure. "Verily the most honoured in the sight of God is the most virtuous amongst you"[7] is applicable to both men and women, to servants and handmaidens. All are under the shadow of the Word of God and all derive their strength from the bounties of the Lord. Therefore, do not consider thyself to be insignificant by doubting what a handmaiden living behind the veil can do. . . .

With a firm heart, a steadfast step and an eloquent tongue arise to spread the Word of God and say: "O God, although I am sitting concealed behind the screen of chastity and am restricted by the veil and exigencies of modesty, my cherished hope is to raise the banner of service and to become a maidservant at Thy Holy Threshold; to ride on a charger and penetrate the army of the ignorant, defeat the mighty regiments and subvert the foundations of error and violation. Thou art the Helper of the weak, Thou art the Sustainer of the poor, Thou art the Succourer of the handmaidens. Verily, Thou art the Almighty and All-Powerful."

(Extract from previously untranslated Tablet)

97. O ye handmaidens who are attracted to the divine fragrances!. . . Confirmations from the kingdom of God will assuredly be received, enabling some radiant leaves to appear resplendent in the assemblage of this world with clear proofs and convincing reasons, which will adorn the cause of womanhood. They will prove that in this cycle women are equal to men, nay in certain respects they will excel. Ponder ye: in this wonderful Cause numerous were the men who scaled the heights of knowledge; they had a brilliant utterance, a convincing proof, an eloquent tongue and magnificent speech, but the blessed leaf, Jináb-i-Ṭáhirih, because she was a woman, emerged with immense splendour and dumbfounded all the people. If she were a man, this would not have been so at all. Therefore, ye should know that the greatness of the Cause hath penetrated the nerves and veins of the world in such wise that if one of the leaves is attracted and gains mastery in demonstrating reasons and proofs and in uttering convincing evidences, she will shine resplendently. O radiant leaves, I swear by the Beauty of the Desired One and the Mystery of Existence that if ye work actively in this realm, the outpourings of the Blessed Beauty will reflect as the sun

---

7. Qur'án 49:13

48

in the mirrors of the hearts. Your progress will astonish all.

The attracted leaves should not, when associating with each other, talk merely about the temperature of the weather, the coldness of the water, the beauty of the flowers and gardens, the freshness of the grass and the flowing water. They should rather restrict their discussions to glorification and praise and the uttering of proofs and reasons, to quoting verses and traditions and putting forth clear testimonies, so that all the homes of the loved ones will be converted into gathering places for lessons on teaching the Cause.

If ye do so, in a short while the outpourings of the Kingdom will be so manifested that each one of the handmaidens of the Merciful will become a perspicuous book revealing the mysteries of the Lord of Mercy. Upon you be the glory of glories.

(Extract from previously untranslated Tablet)

98. In this wondrous Dispensation the favours of the Glorious Lord are vouchsafed unto the handmaidens of the Merciful. Therefore, they should, like unto men, seize the prize and excel in the field, so that it will be proven and made manifest that the penetrative influence of the Word of God in this new Dispensation hath caused women to be equal with men, and that in the arena of tests they will outdo others. Therefore, the true bondsmaids of the Blessed Beauty must be revived by the spirit of detachment, and refreshed by the breezes of attraction, and with hearts overflowing with the love of God, souls gladdened by the heavenly glad-tidings, and with extreme humility and lowliness, let them speak out with eloquent speech, and praise and glorify the Great Lord, for they are the manifestations of such a bounty and adorned with the crown of such splendour.

(Extract from previously untranslated Tablet)

99. O ye pure and esteemed leaves who are nigh to the Court of Glory! Blessed, blessed are ye for ye have arranged spiritual meetings and engaged in propounding divine proofs and evidences. Ye are intent on vindicating truth in support of the manifest Light of the Cause, through conclusive arguments and proofs based on the sacred scriptures of the past. This is a very noble aim, and this cherished hope a cause of the illumination of all peoples and nations.

From the beginning of existence until the present day, in any of the past cycles and dispensations, no assemblies for women have ever been established and classes for the purpose of spreading the teachings were never held by them. This is one of the characteristics of this glorious Dispensation and this great century. Ye should, most certainly, strive to perfect this assemblage and increase your knowledge of the realities of heavenly mysteries, so that, God willing, in a short time, women will become the same as men; they will take a leading position amongst the learned, will each have a fluent tongue and eloquent speech, and shine like unto lamps of guidance throughout the world.In some respects, women have astonishing capacities; they hasten in their attraction to God, and are intense in their fiery ardour for Him. In brief, spend your nights and days in the study of the holy Utterances and in acquiring perfections. Occupy yourselves always in discussing these matters. When ye meet each other, convey the glad-tidings and impart hope to one another because of the confirmations and bounties of the Ancient and Ever-Living Lord. Let each set forth proofs and evidences, and talk about the mysteries of the Kingdom, so that the true and divine Spirit may permeate the body of the contingent world and the secrets of all things, whether of the past or of the future, may become openly manifest and resplendent.

O loved handmaidens of God! Consider not your present merits and capacities, rather fix your gaze on the favours and confirmations of the Blessed Beauty, because His everlasting grace will make of the insignificant plant a blessed tree, will turn the mirage into cool water and wine; will cause the forsaken atom to become the very essence of being, the puny one erudite in the school of knowledge. It enableth a thorny bush to give forth blossoms, and the dark earth to produce fragrant and rich hyacinths. It will transmute the stone into a ruby of great price, and fill the sea shells with brilliant pearls. It will assist a fledgling school child to become a learned teacher and enable a frail embryo to reveal the reality of the verse: "Hallowed be the Lord, the Most Excellent of all creators." [8] Verily, my Lord is powerful over things.

(Extract from previously untranslated Tablet)

100. In this day the duty of everyone, whether man or woman, is to teach the Cause. In America, the women have outdone the men in this regard and have taken the lead in this field. They strive harder in guiding the peoples of the world, and their endeavours are greater. They are confirmed by divine bestowals and blessings. It is my hope that in the East the handmaids of the Merciful will also exert such ef-

---

8. Qur'án 23:14

fort, reveal their powers, and manifest their capacities.
(Extract from previously untranslated Tablet)

101. O virtuous leaf, O teacher of the Cause! Now is the time to speak forth and to deliver speeches, the time to teach and to give testimony. Loosen thy tongue, expound the truths, and establish the validity of the verse: "The All-Merciful hath taught the Qur'án."[9] The Holy Spirit speaketh through the inner-most essence of the human tongue, God's Spirit which desireth communion with the human soul unfoldeth the truths, the Faithful Spirit writeth down and the Spirit of the Ancient of Days confirmeth. I swear by that Peerless Beauty, Who is in the Unseen Kingdom, that when the leaves loose their tongues in praise and glorification of the All-Loving Lord, and in teaching the Cause of the Kind Lord, the concourse of the Kingdom and the inmates of the Unseen Realms will give ear, and cry out with exclamations of extreme joy and jubilation. Glory be upon thee and upon every handmaiden who is steadfast in the Covenant.
(Extract from previously untranslated Tablet)

102. O handmaid of God! . . . To the mothers must be given the divine Teachings and effective counsel, and they must be encouraged and made eager to train their children, for the mother is the first educator of the child. It is she who must, at the very beginning, suckle the new-born at the breast of God's Faith and God's Law, that divine love may enter into him even with his mother's milk, and be with him till his final breath.

So long as the mother faileth to train her children, and start them on a proper way of life, the training which they receive later on will not take its full effect. It is incumbent upon the Spiritual Assemblies to provide the mothers with a well-planned programme for the education of children, showing how, from infancy, the child must be watched over and taught. These instructions must be given to every mother to serve her as a guide, so that each will train and nurture her children in accordance with the Teachings.
(*Selections from the Writings of 'Abdu'l-Bahá*, 1978 World Centre edition, p. 138)

103. . . . we must not make distinctions between individual members of the human family. We must not consider any soul as barren or

___
9. Qur'án 55:2

51

deprived. Our duty lies in educating souls so that the Sun of the bestowals of God shall become resplendent in them, and this is possible through the power of the oneness of humanity. The more love is expressed among mankind and the stronger the power of unity, the greater will be this reflection and revelation, for the greatest bestowal of God is love. Love is the source of all the bestowals of God. Until love takes possession of the heart, no other divine bounty can be revealed in it.

(The Promulgation of Universal Peace, 1982 U.S. edition, p. 15)

104. In brief, the assumption of superiority by man will continue to be depressing to the ambition of woman, as if her attainment to equality was creationally impossible; woman's aspiration toward advancement will be checked by it, and she will gradually become hopeless. On the contrary, we must declare that her capacity is equal, even greater than man's. This will inspire her with hope and ambition, and her susceptibilities for advancement will continually increase. She must not be told and taught that she is weaker and inferior in capacity and qualification. If a pupil is told that his intelligence is less than his fellow pupils, it is a very great drawback and handicap to his progress. He must be encouraged to advance by the statement, ''You are most capable, and if you endeavour, you will attain the highest degree.''

(The Promulgation of Universal Peace, 1982 U.S. edition, pp. 76–77)

105. The purpose, in brief, is this: that if woman be fully educated and granted her rights, she will attain the capacity for wonderful accomplishments and prove herself the equal of man. She is the coadjutor of man, his complement and helpmeet.

(The Promulgation of Universal Peace, 1982 U.S. edition, p. 136)

106. The realities of things have been revealed in this radiant century, and that which is true must come to the surface. Among these realities is the principle of the equality of man and woman—equal rights and prerogatives in all things appertaining to humanity. Bahá'u'lláh declared this reality over fifty years ago. But while this principle of equality is true, it is likewise true that woman must prove her capacity and aptitude, must show forth the evidences of equali-

ty. She must become proficient in the arts and sciences and prove by her accomplishments that her abilities and powers have merely been latent. Demonstrations of force, such as are now taking place in England, are neither becoming nor effective in the cause of womanhood and equality. Woman must especially devote her energies and abilities toward the industrial and agricultural sciences, seeking to assist mankind in that which is most needful. By this means she will demonstrate capability and ensure recognition of equality in the social and economic equation. Undoubtedly God will confirm her in her efforts and endeavours, for in this century of radiance Bahá'u'lláh has proclaimed the reality of the oneness of the world of humanity and announced that all nations, peoples and races are one.
(*The Promulgation of Universal Peace*, 1982
U.S. edition, pp. 283-284)

107. Equality of the sexes will be established in proportion to the increased opportunities afforded woman in this age, for man and woman are equally the recipients of powers and endowments from God, the Creator. God has not ordained distinction between them in His consummate purpose.
(*The Promulgation of Universal Peace*, 1982
U.S. edition, p. 300)

108. Woman must endeavour then to attain greater perfection, to be man's equal in every respect, to make progress in all in which she has been backward, so that man will be compelled to acknowledge her equality of capacity and attainment.

In Europe women have made greater progress than in the East, but there is still much to be done! When students have arrived at the end of their school term an examination takes place, and the result thereof determines the knowledge and capacity of each student. So will it be with woman; her actions will show her power, there will no longer be any need to proclaim it by words.

It is my hope that women of the East, as well as their Western sisters, will progress rapidly until humanity shall reach perfection.

God's Bounty is for all and gives power for all progress. When men own the equality of women there will be no need for them to struggle for their rights! One of the principles then of Bahá'u'lláh is the equality of sex.

Women must make the greatest effort to acquire spiritual power and to increase in the virtue of wisdom and holiness until their

53

enlightenment and striving succeeds in bringing about the unity of mankind. They must work with a burning enthusiasm to spread the Teaching of Bahá'u'lláh among the peoples, so that the radiant light of the Divine Bounty may envelop the souls of all the nations of the world!

(*Paris Talks*, 1961 U.K. edition, pp. 162–163)

Extracts from Letters Written by the Guardian:

109. Regarding the position of the Bahá'í women in India and Burma, and their future collaboration with the men in the administrative work of the Cause, I feel that the time is now ripe that those women who have already conformed to the prevailing custom in India and Burma by discarding the veil should not only be given the right to vote for the election of their local and national representatives, but should themselves be eligible to the membership of all Bahá'í Assemblies throughout India and Burma, be they local or national.

This definite and most important step, however, should be taken with the greatest care and caution, prudence and thoughtfulness. Due regard must be paid to their actual capacity and present attainments, and only those who are best qualified for membership, be they men or women, and irrespective of social standing, should be elected to the extremely responsible position of a member of the Bahá'í Assembly.

This momentous decision, I trust, will prove to be a great incentive to the women Bahá'ís throughout India and Burma who, I hope, will now bestir themselves and endeavour to the best of their ability to acquire a better and more profound knowledge of the Cause, to take a more active and systematic part in the general affairs of the Movement, and prove themselves in every way enlightened, responsible and efficient co-workers to their fellow-men in their common task for the advancement of the Cause throughout their country. May they fully realize their high responsibilities in this day, may they do all in their power to justify the high hopes we cherish for their future, and may they prove themselves in every respect worthy of the noble mis-

sion which the Bahá'í world is now entrusting to their charge.
(27 December 1923 to a National Spiritual
Assembly)

110. Full rights have been accorded to Bahá'í women residing in the cradle of the Faith, to participate in the membership of both national and local Bahá'í Spiritual Assemblies, removing thereby the last remaining obstacle to the enjoyment of complete equality of rights in the conduct of the administrative affairs of the Persian Bahá'í Community.
(April 1954 *Messages to the Bahá'í World*, 1971
U.S. edition, p. 65)

111. That the members of this community [American], of either sex and of every age, of whatever race or background, however limited in experience, capacity and knowledge, may arise as one man, and seize with both hands the God-given opportunities now presented to them through the dispensations of an all-loving, ever-watchful, ever-sustaining Providence, and lend thereby a tremendous impetus to the propelling forces mysteriously guiding the operations of this newly launched, unspeakably potent, world-encompassing Crusade, is one of the dearest wishes which a loving and longing heart holds for them at this great turning point in the fortunes of the Faith of Bahá'u'lláh in the American continent.
(28 July 1954, *Citadel of Faith*, 1980
U.S. edition, p. 132)

Extracts from Letters and a Telex
Written by the Universal House of Justice:

112. Concerning the point you raised in your letter. . . that the women's liberation movement in. . . is assuming extreme positions which are having some influence on impressionable Bahá'í young women, we feel it would be helpful if your Assembly were to stress the unique position that women occupy by being members of the

Bahá'í Faith particularly through participation in the administration of its affairs on both a local and national scale.
(9 April 1971 to a National Spiritual Assembly)

113. 'Abdu'l-Bahá has pointed out that "Among the miracles which distinguish this sacred Dispensation is this, that women have evinced a greater boldness than men when enlisted in the ranks of the Faith." Shoghi Effendi has further stated that this "boldness" must, in the course of time, "be more convincingly demonstrated, and win for the beloved Cause victories more stirring than any it has as yet achieved." Although obviously the entire Bahá'í world is committed to encouraging and stimulating the vital rôle of women in the Bahá'í community as well as in society at large, the Five Year Plan calls specifically on eighty National Spiritual Assemblies to organize Bahá'í activities for women. In the course of the current year which has been designated "International Women's Year" as a world-wide activity of the United Nations, the Bahá'ís, particularly in these eighty national communities, should initiate and implement programs which will stimulate and promote the full and equal participation of women in all aspects of Bahá'í community life, so that through their accomplishments the friends will demonstrate the distinction of the Cause of God in this field of human endeavour.
(25 May 1975 to all National Spiritual Assemblies)

114. PARTICULARLY CALL UPON BAHÁ'Í WOMEN, WHOSE CAPACITIES IN MANY LANDS STILL LARGELY UNUSED, AND WHOSE POTENTIAL FOR SERVICE CAUSE SO GREAT, TO ARISE AND DEMONSTRATE IMPORTANCE PART THEY ARE TO PLAY IN ALL FIELDS SERVICE FAITH.
(24 March 1977 telex to a National
Spiritual Assembly)

115. The youth have long been in the forefront of the teaching work, and now our hearts rejoice to see the women, in so many lands where previously their capacities were largely left unused, devoting their capable services to the life of the Bahá'í community.
(Riḍván 1978)

116. At the heart of all activities, the spiritual, intellectual and community life of the believers must be developed and fostered, requiring: the prosecution with increased vigour of the development of

56

Local Spiritual Assemblies so that they may exercise their beneficial influence and guidance on the life of Bahá'í communities; the nurturing of a deeper understanding of Bahá'í family life; the Bahá'í education of children, including the holding of regular Bahá'í classes and, where necessary, the establishment of tutorial schools for the provision of elementary education; the encouragement of Bahá'í youth in study and service; and the encouragement of Bahá'í women to exercise to the full their privileges and responsibilities in the work of the community—may they befittingly bear witness to the memory of the Greatest Holy Leaf, the immortal heroine of the Bahá'í Dispensation, as we approach the fiftieth anniversary of her passing.
(Naw-Rúz 1979)

117. The equality of men and women is not, at the present time, universally applied. In those areas where traditional inequality still hampers its progress we must take the lead in practicing this Bahá'í principle. Bahá'í women and girls must be encouraged to take part in the social, spiritual and administrative activities of their communities.
(Riḍván 1984)

118. Calling upon local and national Bahá'í communities to sponsor a wide range of activities which will engage the attention of people from all walks of life to various topics relevant to peace, such as: the role of women, ...
(23 January 1985 to all National Spiritual Assemblies)

Extracts from Letters Written on Behalf of the Universal House of Justice:

119. The House of Justice regards the need to educate and guide women in their primary responsibility as mothers as an excellent opportunity for organizing women's activities. Your efforts should focus on helping them in their function as educators of the rising generation.
(29 February 1984 to a National Spiritual Assembly)

120. The principle of the equality between women and men, like the other teachings of the Faith, can be effectively and universally established among the friends when it is pursued in conjunction with all the other aspects of Bahá'í life. Change is an evolutionary process requiring patience with one's self and others, loving education and the passage of time as the believers deepen their knowledge of the principles of the Faith, gradually discard long-held traditional attitudes and progressively conform their lives to the unifying teachings of the Cause.

(25 July 1984 to an individual believer)

Bibliography

Bahá'u'lláh. *The Hidden Words*. London: National Spiritual Assembly of the British Isles, 1949.

————. *Tablets of Bahá'u'lláh revealed after the Kitáb-i-Aqdas*. Haifa: Bahá'í World Centre, 1978.

'Abdu'l-Bahá. *Selections from the Writings of 'Abdu'l-Bahá*. Haifa: Bahá'í World Centre, 1978.

————. *The Promulgation of Universal Peace*. Wilmette: Bahá'í Publishing Trust, 1982.

————. *Paris Talks*. London: Bahá'í Publishing Trust, 1961.

————. *'Abdu'l-Bahá in London*. London: Bahá'í Publishing Trust, 1982.

Shoghi Effendi. *Messages to the Bahá'í World, 1950–1957*. Wilmette: Bahá'í Publishing Trust, 1971.

————. *Citadel of Faith*. Wilmette: Bahá'í Publishing Trust, 1980.

Bahá'í Education, A Compilation. Haifa: Bahá'í World Centre, 1976.

Family Life. London: Bahá'í Publishing Trust, 1982.

Abdul Baha on Divine Philosophy, compiled by Isobel F. Chamberlain, Boston: The Tudor Press, 1917.

Esslemont, John Ebenezer. *Bahá'u'lláh and the New Era*, Wilmette: Bahá'í Publishing Trust, 1976.